A Cold Night In February

By Mike Platt

Illustrations:
James Bennett

©2024 Michael Platt
ISBN 979-8-35098-403-3
All rights reserved.

It was a cold night in February as fans gathered for the big game.

Generation after generation passing down their love of the team.

Wishing for a championship,
a city united in its dream.

This season felt different.
The birds inspiring hope and belief.

Overcoming many challenges
to put the dream within reach.

The game finally kicked off.
And they got off to a great start!

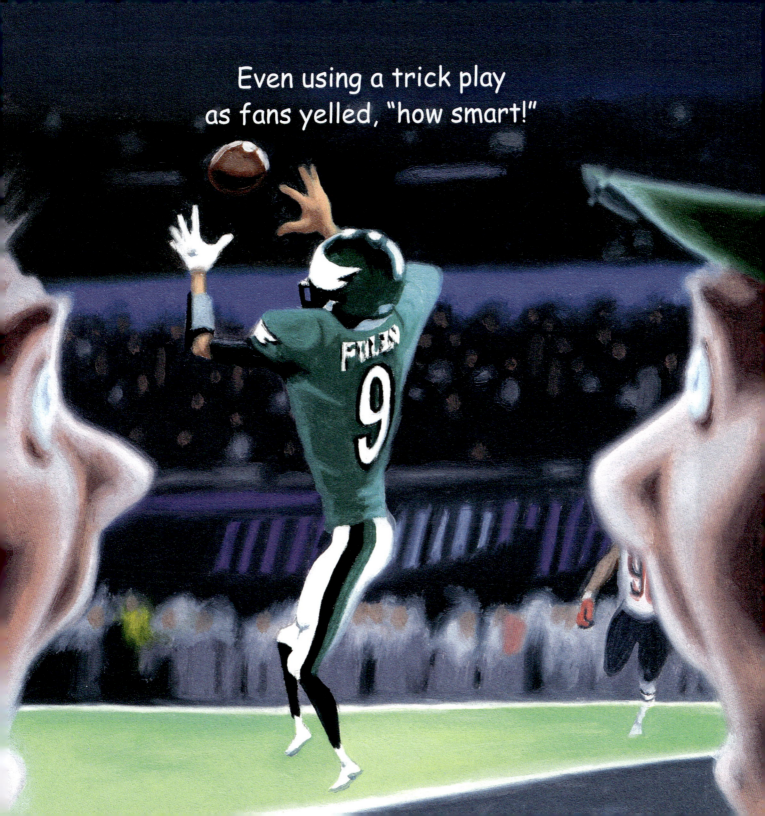

As the second half began the birds led by ten.

It's times like these
when doubt starts to creep in.

But those who keep believing
get most rewarded in the end.

As the clock ticked down
the birds needed a big play.

And before the fans knew it
they had taken the ball away!

With just one more stop the players would be heroes.

And as the hail mary hit the ground
the clock struck double zeroes.

It had finally happened.
What some thought might never.
The birds were the champs!
A feeling as good as ever.

Fans started to think back to the hard times they'd gone through.

When they wondered if it was all worth it. If they'd ever get this good mood.

But what they learned was that hope doesn't have to be scary.

Because you never know what can happen...

...on a cold night in February.

Mike Platt is a passionate and optimistic Philadelphia sports fan who believes there are positive lessons we can teach our children through our experiences as fans.

He resides in Bucks County, Pennsylvania with his wife and daughters.